Masonic Life of George Washington

By

Albert G. Mackey

Copyright © 2020 Lamp of Trismegistus. All rights reserved. No part of this publication may be reproduced or transmitted in any form or by any means, electronic or mechanical, including photocopying, recording, or by any information storage and retrieval system, without permission in writing from Lamp of Trismegistus. Reviewers may quote brief passages.

ISBN: 978-1-63118-457-4

*Foundations of Freemasonry
Series*

Other Books in this Series and Related Titles

The Mysteries of Freemasonry & the Druids
by Albert G. Mackey, Manly P. Hall, &c (978-1-63118-444-4)

Royal Arch, Capitular and Cryptic Masonry
by various authors (978-1-63118-425-3)

Masonic Symbolism of Easter and the Christ in Masonry
by various authors (978-1-63118-434-5)

Masonic Symbolism of King Solomon's Temple
by Albert G. Mackey, David Harlow & Robert Smailes
(978-1-63118-442-0)

The Kabbalah of Masonry & Related Writings
by W. W. Westcott, Eliphas Levi &c (978-1-63118-453-6)

The Two Great Pillars of Boaz and Jachin
by Albert G. Mackey, William Harvey &c (978-1-63118-433-8)

Masonic Symbolism of the Apron & the Altar
by various authors (978-1-63118-428-4)

The Regius Poem or Halliwell Manuscript
by King Solomon (978-1-63118-447-5)

Freemasonry in the Medieval or Middle Ages
by R. I. Clegg & C. W. Leadbeater (978-1-63118-450-5)

Symbolism and Discourses on the Entered Apprentice, Fellowcraft and Master Mason Blue Lodge Degrees by various (978-1-63118-413-0)

The Lost Keys of Freemasonry or The Secret of Hiram Abiff
by Manly P. Hall (978-1-63118-427-7)

The Story and Legend of Hiram Abiff by William Harvey, Manly P. Hall & Albert G. Mackey (978-1-63118-411-6)

Audio Versions are also Available on Audible and iTunes

Table of Contents

Introduction...9

Washington as a Freemason
by Albert G. Mackey...11

The Testimony of President George Washington...31

George Washington: An Acrostic...37

Appendix 1:
The Testimony of President John Adams...39

Appendix 2:
The Testimony of President Andrew Jackson...41

Appendix 3:
The Masonic Presidents...43

Introduction

From the beginning of Modern Freemasonry's birthdate of 1717, the intelligentsia of humanity have found refuge for safe reflection within the walls of the fraternity. Masonic writers have produced a nearly incalculable amount of written musings on a multitude of esoteric and philosophical subjects, as they relate to the ancient mysteries that Freemasonry currently storehouses. Sadly, most of it appears to have sat largely unread, as American Freemasonry in particular, continues to transform itself into something that bears little resemblance to what it was originally designed to be. The true essence of Freemasonry is not that of blind patriotism or a single-minded national religion but one of Universal Brotherhood and altruism, designed for the betterment not just of its members but of society as a whole. In particular, for those who are not members of the fraternity, as Freemasonry has always acted as a beacon, to help guide humanity through darker times, with the hopes that one day we will collectively reach a truly enlightened age.

It's not uncommon for new members joining the fraternity to find little education within the walls of many modern lodges, in spite of so much written material available to the membership. Many older members are not simply uneducated with regards to real Masonic history and symbology, not to mention the vast arena of related subjects, but they are disinterested in all of it, as well.

Lamp of Trismegistus is doing its part to help preserve humanity's Masonic history by making some of these classics available to those students who are seeking to unearth the knowledge of these ancient colossi. As such, Lamp of Trismegistus offers its readers highlights of Masonic study, culled from a variety of authors and viewpoints, with the hope bringing education back into the fraternity. So, be sure to check out other titles in our *Foundations of Freemasonry Series* as well as our *Esoteric Classics, Theosophical Classics, Occult Fiction, Paranormal Classics, Supernatural Fiction* and our *Christian Apocrypha Series*, and don't be afraid to let a little altruism into your own heart or even into your Lodge. You can also download the audio versions of most of these titles from iTunes or Audible, for learning on the go.

Washington as a Freemason

By Albert G. Mackey

Delivered by Albert G. Mackey, M. D., Grand Secretary and Grand Lecturer of the Grand Lodge of South Carolina; General of the Supreme Council of the 33rd degree, for the Southern Jurisdiction of the United States, etc., etc., before the Grand and subordinate lodges of Ancient Freemasons of South Carolina, at Charleston, South Carolina, on Thursday, November 4, 1852, being the centennial celebration of the initiation of George Washington.

One hundred years ago - the day which we are now celebrating with all these public demonstrations of joy and pride - and which tens of thousands of our brethren are commemorating with us, in every city and town and village throughout the length and breadth of this vast empire - was hallowed in the history of the Masonic institution, by the initiation into its sublime mysteries of the Father of his Country.

The scenes enacted on that day in a small and obscure lodge of the Old Dominion were then, while the dark veil of the futurity was still undrawn, supposed to be of an ordinary character. The minute book of the Lodge at Fredericksburg presents no more than the usual record, that on the 4th of November, 1752, George Washington was initiated as an Entered Apprentice. The youth, who, though even then he had been honored by a distinguished appointment in the military service of his native State, had not yet developed the germ of his future greatness, passed undoubtedly through the solemn ceremonies of initiation into our mystic rites, without any suspicion on the part of those who assisted in bestowing on him the light of Masonry, that the transaction then occurring was to become an era in the annals of our institution, and that a century afterwards their descendants would ordain a jubilee, to hail its memory with shouts of joy and to celebrate its anniversary with loud peans of praise. But time, whose lessons are always progressive and often unexpected, has since taught us that the event of that evening was among the most important in the history of American Masonry. It has furnished a topic of angry discussion to the enemies, and of grateful exultation to the friends, of our institution. It has given an abiding testimony of the virtuous principles of that society, among whose disciples "the patriot, the hero and the sage" did not disdain to be numbered. And while time shall last and Masonry shall endure, that old but distinctly legible page in the record book of Fredericksburg Lodge will be pointed to with proud satisfaction by every Mason, as indisputable evidence that the wisest of statesmen, the purest of patriots, the most virtuous of men, was indeed his brother and bound with him in one common but mystic tie of fraternity and love.

In the ancient record book of the Lodge at Fredericksburg in Virginia - a book venerable for its age as a relic of the past - but still more venerable for the pages on which the record is made, will be found the following entries.

The first entry is thus:

No. 4th, 1752. This evening Mr. George Washington was initiated as an Entered Apprentice," and the receipt of the entrance fee, amounting to 2 pounds 3s is acknowledged.

On the 3rd of March in the following year, "Mr. George Washington" is recorded as having been passed a Fellow Craft; and on the 4th of the succeeding August the transactions of the evening are that "Mr. George Washington," and others whose names are mentioned, are stated to have been raised to the sublime degree of Master Mason.

These records of the early Masonic career of Washington are inestimable to the Mason as memorials of the first connection of the Father of his Country with our institution. But if the history of that connection had there ceased; if admitted to our temple, he had but glanced with cold and indifferent eye upon its mysteries; and if then, unaffected by their beauty - untouched by their sublimity, and unwakened by their truth, lie had departed from our portals - the pride with which we hail him as a brother would have been a vain presumption, and the celebration of this day, a senseless mockery. But the seed of Masonry which was sown on the evening of that November fell not on a barren soil. It grew with his growth and strengthened with his strength, and bloomed and ripened into an abiding love and glowing zeal for our order, nor ever withered or decayed amid all the trials and struggles, the perils and excitement of a long life spent, first in battling to gain the liberties of his country, and then in counseling to preserve them.

The evidence of all this is on record, and the genuineness of the record cannot be disputed. Whatever the enemies of Masonry may say to the contrary - however they may have attempted in the virulence of their persecution, to insinuate that his connection with our order was but accidental and temporary - first formed in the thoughtlessness of youth and then at once and forever dissolved - there is abundant testimony to show that he never for a moment disowned his allegiance to the mystic art - and never omitted, on every appropriate occasion, by active participation in our rites, to vindicate the purity of the institution and to demonstrate in the most public manner, his respect for its principles.

Years after his initiation, when he held the exalted rank of leader of our armies in those deeply perilous days, which have been so well defined as "the times that tried men's souls," notwithstanding his responsible duties, his arduous labors, his mental disquietudes, he would often lay aside the ensigns of his supreme authority, and forgetting for a time "the pomp and circumstance of glorious war," would enter the secluded tent and mingle on a level with his brave companions, in the solemn devotions and mystic rites of some military lodge, where, under the sacred influence of Masonry, the god of carnage found no libations poured upon his altar, but where the heartfelt prayer for the prevalence of harmony and brotherly love was offered to the Grand Architect of the Universe. We have the authority of a distinguished Mason of Virginia, who has elaborately investigated the Masonic life of Washington, for saying that *"frequently, when surrounded by a brilliant staff, he would part from the gay assemblage and seek the instruction of the Lodge."* And there was actually living in Ohio a few years ago a revolutionary veteran, Captain Hugh Maloy, who on one of these occasions was initiated in the marquee of Washington, the Commander in Chief himself presiding at the ceremony.

In scenes like these, the great Napoleon has been known to appear, and the lodges of Paris have more than once beheld the ruler of the empire mingling in their labors, a willing witness of the great doctrine of Masonic equality. But in the founder of a new dynasty, such condescension might - and possibly with some truth - be attributed to the policy of winning popular applause. In our truehearted, single-minded Washington, no such subservience to man-worship could be suspected. His only motives were deep love for the institution, and profound admiration of its principles.

Permit me, before we proceed to a review of the later portions of Washington's Masonic life, to invite your attention to one, other revolutionary incident, reflecting equal honor upon the subject of our address, and on the order of which he was so illustrious a member.

A distinguished brother who faithfully and valiantly served his country, in the last contest in which it has been engaged, once remarked, in an address delivered by him before the Grand Lodge of this State, that much as he admired Masonry it was only on the field of battle that he had really learned to love it. Wisely and truthfully were those words uttered. For it is there, amid loud hosannas to the god of slaughter, when

> "*Men with rage and hate*
> *Make war upon their kind,*
> *And the land is fed by the blood they shed, In their lust for*
> *carnage blind,*"

that the voice of Masonry speaks in tones that are heard above the dull booming of artillery, and the shrill blast of the bugle. It is there, when the utterance of humanity is hushed - when language, created by its beneficent author, to express man's wants and man's affections, is exchanged for the clashing of steel - when the plunge of the bayonet or the thrust of the saber is too often the only reply to the cry for mercy - and when human sympathy has been driven from its throne in the human heart - it is there that the whispered word may make its strong appeal, and the mute yet eloquent sign, will paralyze the uplifted arm, converting by its hidden necromancy, hate into love, and binding in a moment the conqueror and the conquered with these strong cords of fraternal affection which will withstand the utmost strain of national enmity to snap asunder.

Scenes and events of this kind were of course occurring in our revolutionary war - for there is no contest among civilized nations in which they are not present. But one in which Washington was more particularly and immediately engaged may serve to show how perfectly he understood and appreciated this beautiful feature in the Masonic system.

In the forty-sixth regiment of the British army there was a traveling Lodge, holding its Warrant of Constitution under the jurisdiction of the Grand Lodge of Ireland. After an engagement between the American and British forces, in which the latter were defeated, the private chest of the Lodge, containing its jewels, furniture and implements, fell into the hands of the Americans. The captors reported the circumstances to General Washington, who at once ordered the chest to be returned to the Lodge and the regiment, under a guard of honor. "The surprise," says the historian of the event, himself an Englishman and a Mason,

> *"the feeling of both officers and men may be imagined, when they perceived the flag of truce that announced this elegant compliment from their noble opponent, but still more noble brother. The guard of honor, with their music playing a sacred march - the chest containing the Constitution and implements of the Craft borne aloft, like another ark of the covenant, equally by Englishmen and Americans, who lately engaged in the strife of war, now marched through the enfiladed ranks of the gallant regiment that, with presented arms and colors, hailed the glorious act by cheers, which the sentiment rendered sacred as the hallelujahs of an angel's song."*

When the contest which secured the independence and freedom of his country was terminated, Washington, covered with the admiration and gratitude of his fellow citizens, retired like another Cincinnatus to the shades of private life. But he did not abandon then his interest in the institution of which he was an honored member.

In 1788 he united with others in presenting a petition for the formation of a new Lodge at Alexandria, and the Warrant of Constitution, as the instrument authorizing the organization is technically called, is still in existence, preserved in the archives of that Lodge, and has been seen by thousands.

That Warrant commences with these words - words which now cannot be altogether heard with cold indifference:

"I, Edmund Randolph, Governor of the State, and Grand Master of the Grand Lodge of Virginia, do hereby constitute and appoint our illustrious and well-beloved Brother

George Washington, late General and Commander-in-Chief of the forces of the United States of America, and our worthy Brothers Robert McCrea, William Hunter, Jr., and Joseph Allison, Esq., together with all such other brethren as may be admitted to associate with them, to be a just, true and regular Lodge of Freemasons, by the name, title and designation of Alexandria Lodge, No. 22."

The Lodge is still in existence and in active operation, but in 1805 it changed its name in honor of its first Master to that of "Washington Alexandria."

No one acquainted with the character of Washington - with his indomitable energy, his scrupulous punctuality, and his rigid adherence to method in business, will for a moment suppose that he would ever have engaged in a labor which he did not ardently strive to accomplish, or have accepted an office whose duties he did not conscientiously discharge. But his general and well-known reputation for these virtues is not all that we possess as a testimony of the mode in which he met the responsible cares of presiding over the Craft.

The Hon. Timothy Bigelow, in an eulogy delivered before the Grand Lodge of Massachusetts, two months after Washington's death, when there were still living witnesses of his Masonic life, with whom the speaker had conversed, supplies us on this point with the following evidence:

"The information received from our brethren who had the happiness to be members of the Lodge over which he presided for many years, and of which he died the Master, furnishes abundant proof of his persevering zeal for

the prosperity of the institution. Constant and punctual in his attendance, scrupulous in his observance of the regulations of the Lodge, and solicitous at all times to communicate light and instruction, he discharged the duties of the chair with uncommon dignity and intelligence in all the mysteries of our art."

Incidents like these, interesting as they may be, are not all that is left to us to exhibit the attachment of Washington to Masonry. On repeated occasions he has announced, in his letters and addresses to various Masonic bodies, his profound esteem for the character and his just appreciation of the principles of that institution into which, at so early an age, he had been admitted. And during his long and laborious life, no opportunity was presented of which he did not gladly avail himself to evince that he was a Mason in heart as well as in name.

Thus, in the year 1797, in reply to an affectionate address from the Grand Lodge of Massachusetts, he says: *"My attachment to the Society of which we are members will dispose me always to contribute my best endeavors to promote the honor and prosperity of the Craft."*

Five years before this letter was written, he had, in a communication to the same body, expressed his opinion of the Masonic institution as one whose liberal principles are founded on the immutable laws of "truth and justice," and whose "grand object is to promote the happiness of the human race."

In answer to an address from the Grand Lodge of South Carolina in 1791, he says: "I recognize, with pleasure, my relation to the brethren of your Society," and "I shall be happy, on every occasion, to evince my regard for the fraternity." And in the same letter he takes occasion to allude to the Masonic institution as "an association whose principles lead to purity of morals and are beneficial of action."

In writing to the officers and members of St. David's Lodge, at Newport, R. I., in the same year, he uses this language:

"Being persuaded that a just application of the principles on which the Masonic fraternity is founded must be promotive of private virtue and public prosperity, I shall always be happy to advance the interests of the Society, and to be considered by them as a deserving brother."

And lastly, for we will not further extend these quotations, in a letter addressed in November, 1798, only thirteen months before his death, to the Grand Lodge of Maryland, he has made this explicit declaration of his opinion of the Institution:

"So far as I am acquainted with the doctrines and principles of Freemasonry, I conceive them to be founded in benevolence, and to be exercised only for the good of mankind. I cannot, therefore, upon this ground, withdraw my approbation from it."

If I have paused thus long upon these memorials of the past, and if I have borrowed thus largely from these evidences of Washington's opinions, it is that, so far as this audience at least is affected, the question of his attachment to our Order may be forever put to rest, and that the falsehoods and forgeries of our enemies may be detected by a reference to the authentic expressions in our favor of the very man whom they have published to the world as the enemy of Freemasonry. Henceforth the words which have been uttered here today - to some of you undoubtedly familiar, but by many now heard for the first time - will stand as incontrovertible evidence that Washington was, in very truth, a Mason - in heart, in affection and in allegiance. Not merely in name and in outward bearing, but one who wrought with us in our hours of labor, and whose visits to our temple were prompted by no idle curiosity, but by a warm devotion to the interests of the Craft, and a philosophical admiration of our mystic system.

And is it not a noble eulogy of our institution that it should have numbered among its faithful disciples one so stainless in morals, so devout in religion, a patriot so pure, a statesman so virtuous, that his life was the admiration of the world - his death, the desolation of his country?

There is, indeed, in the whole pervading spirit of Freemasonry something of that "beauty of holiness" which must have been congenial to the character of such a man as he. His heart was irresistibly drawn to it by the purity of its principles, and the sublime beneficence of its design. He could not but love, because it was holy, and he could not but admire it, because it was intellectual.

Though I will not undertake to say that Washington was indebted for any of those beautiful traits which adorned his character, to the influence of Masonic teaching (*because I know that he derived them from a more divine school*), yet there was undoubtedly such a similarity in the most prominent virtues that illustrated his life to those which constitute the very ground work of the Masonic system, as must have readily won from him respect and esteem for our institution.

Unfaltering Trust in God - an humble dependence on the wisdom and power of the Supreme Controller of the Universe - is the first as well as the most indispensable moral qualification of every candidate for our mystic rites. And this virtue, the foundation and suggester of every other, was a distinguishing feature in the religious constitution of Washington. In all his private and public letters, in his official correspondence with the government, and in his orders to the army, this firm reliance - this trustful dependence on Divine Providence is prominently and frequently referred to as though it were a topic on which he could not too often dilate.

Of Charity, which has been aptly called the cap-stone of the Masonic edifice, and which, like the virtue already spoken of, is taught in the most important ceremonies of initiation, Washington was an illustrious example. Throughout his life he sought rather for opportunities of discharging the claims of his virtue than for apologies for its neglect, and he uniformly acted whenever the poor and the deserving were presented to his notice under the influence of that great doctrine of our Order, which teaches us "to soothe the unhappy; to sympathize with their misfortunes; to compassionate their miseries, and to restore peace to their troubled minds."

And again, Brotherly Love, that sublime principle of philanthropy, by which, as it is defined in our ritual, *"we are taught to regard the whole human species as one family; the high and low, the rich and poor; who, as created by one Almighty Parent, are to aid, support and protect each other"* - was admirably exemplified in his humanity to the prisoner, his condescension to his inferiors, his warm friendship, his general benevolence, and his uniform urbanity and gentleness of manner to all who approached him. His was indeed the character to win kindness from an enemy, or to secure fidelity in a friend.

The Cardinal Virtues, too, so beautifully inculcated in the lectures of our system, were eminently prominent in the character of our beloved brother. And when the neophyte of our order, standing before the Pedestal of the East, is receiving from the Master of the Lodge those deeply significant symbols by which these virtues are to be impressed upon his mind and heart, I know not where better the teacher could seek for a bright example of Temperance than in him who ever placed a due restraint upon the passions of his humanity, and whose mind was thus proverbially freed from the allurements of vice - or of Fortitude, than in him whose noble purposes of soul enabled him to undergo for the good of his country every peril, pain and danger that beset his path - or of Prudence, than in him whose whole life was regulated by the dictates of reason and who was not more a Fabius in the field than he was a Solon in the cabinet - or of justice, than in him who, in the administration of both private and public affairs, always accorded to every man his just due, without distinction of rank or person.

And lastly, as to that other great Masonic virtue, Truth, the "divine attribute," which, as Masons, we are taught constantly to contemplate, and by which we are directed to regulate our conduct - where or when lived the man who, from his very infancy, was more influenced than he by this holy principle; or of whom we might more truthfully say that his soul was its throne - his whole life its active embodiment?

But why extend the catalogue, or why protract this eulogium of him whom now to praise were indeed "to paint the lily or to gild refined gold." If on the tomb of the great architect of St. Paul's, lying beneath the magnificent dome of that proud temple which his own genius had created, it was thought all sufficient to inscribe this epitaph: "If you would seek his monument, look around!" - may we not, viewing this goodly audience and this large assemblage of the members of a mystic fraternity, offering up the holocaust of their whole heart's veneration - and that, too, not here alone, but in all the widely separated segments of this vast empire - in the North, in the South, in the East, and the West - all animated by one common feeling of joyous exultation that the most loved and honored of our might dead - was with us and of us - bound willingly and cheerfully to himself in our bond of fraternity - looking thus at all that is around us, in this public display, and all that is in us and about us, in the sentiment of honest pride, that as Masons warms and animates us - may we not point to this day and to these services as a "monument more perennial than brass" of our own - our venerated brother.

The fact that Washington was an active and devoted member of our fraternity is in itself a source to us of gratulation, because it furnishes unanswerable testimony (*as one of the ablest of our opponents has candidly admitted*) that "there is nothing in the institution at war with our duties as patriots, men and Christians." But, while we thus peculiarly honor the greatest man of his age, and assert that in uniting with us he vindicated by his own virtue the purity of his principles, we may be permitted to indulge in the consoling consciousness that such a vindication was not altogether wanting; but that both before and since the connection of Washington with the Craft the history of Freemasonry has presented a catalogue of glorious names inscribed upon its proud escutcheon. It is indeed with truth that the ritual of our Order declares to each initiate that *"the greatest and best of men in all ages have been encouragers and promoters of the art, and have never deemed it derogatory to their dignity to level themselves with the fraternity, to extend their privileges and to patronize their assemblies."* Without directing our researches into that remote antiquity whose consideration would involve us in too elaborate an inquiry, I may be permitted to remind the scholar and the antiquary that during the medieval ages the art of ecclesiastical architecture was carried by the Freemasons to that state of classic beauty and scientific perfection that has never since been equaled by the builders of succeeding times - that the invention and the most gorgeous examples of the pointed gothic are attributable to our Masonic ancestors - and that throughout the whole of Europe, from the south of Italy to the north of Scotland, cathedrals, abbeys and churches lift their tall and graceful spires as monuments of the skill and ingenuity of the fraternity - or in their magnificent ruins, still "beautiful in death," continue to extort the admiration of modern taste or to defy the rivalry of the modern art.

It was then that Popes and Bishops, Kings and Nobles, lavished their patronage on our Order, and vied with each other in the protection and encouragement of the institution. And although at a subsequent period the church, from motives into whose character I will not now stop to inquire, withdrew its friendly countenance, and in still later years commenced a series of unsuccessful persecutions, many notwithstanding, of the good and wise, the great and the powerful in every age and country, have been found among the disciples of our mystic school.

It is indeed with somewhat more than ordinary pride and gratulation that we claim as our brethren, among a host of others, such men as Sir Christopher Wren, the builder of St. Paul's - and Sir Thomas Gresham, the founder of the Royal Exchange, the princely gift to London of one of London's merchant princes - and Elias Ashmole, one of the most learned of English antiquarians - and Helvetius, the profound philosopher and mighty thinker - and Lalande, the celebrated astronomer of France - and Goethe and Schiller, the immortal masters of German poesy - and Sir Walter Scott, the great magician of the North - and Horsely, the distinguished Bishop of Rochester, who boldly stood up in the British Parliament to defend, when assailed, that fraternity of which he proudly announced himself to be a member - and Sir William Follet, the learned and exemplary lawyer and the late Attorney General of England, who did not hesitate to declare his attachment to our institution, and to assign, as a reason for that attachment, "the kindly sympathy and widespread benevolence and cordial love" its system created.

And the potentates of earth have knelt at our altar and breathed forth our vows. Frederick the Great of Prussia, and George IV of England, with all his uncles and brothers, and Oscar of Sweden, and Christian of Denmark, and Ernest of Hanover, may be named among the many kings and princes who have not only been the patrons, but the disciples of our art.

And Napoleon, with every marshal and general of Napoleon's camp; and Nelson and Wellington, whose ashes are not yet inured, and Collingwood and Napier, and every distinguished leader of England's army and navy, have worn the Mason's badge, and learned the Mason's sign.

In our country the roll of distinguished Masons is not less honorable to the fraternity. In the revolutionary war all the generals of the American army, both the children of our own soil and those noble and kindred spirits who came from France and Germany and Poland to assist us, were bound together, not only by the glorious bond of common struggle, but by the additional cords of Masonic fraternity. And when in after days, La Fayette, that patriot of two hemispheres, had returned to the home from which for our cause, he had so long been an exile, he could find no more appropriate token of his grateful recollection to convey to Washington, his venerated father in arms, than a Mason's scarf and a Mason's apron, and which, wrought by Madam La Fayette, a Mason's wife, were long treasured and worn by him to whom they were presented, and are now preserved as sacred relics by the Lodge at Alexandria.

In civil life we claim an equally noble catalogue. More than fifty of the signers of the Declaration of Independence, several of our Presidents and judges, and many of our most distinguished statesmen, have been initiated into the rites of Masonry.

Franklin, the chief of our philosophers, and Griswold, one of the most pious of our prelates, and Clinton, the purest of our patriots, showed by their steadfast attachment to our institution their just appreciation of its principles; and Henry Clay, that man of immoral mind, whose death his country is still lamenting, is recorded in our annals as a Mason of unfaltering devotion, who, years ago, sacrificed the aspirations of ambition to his love of the Craft and refused a nomination for the Presidency by what was then supposed to be a powerful party, when the price of his support was to be a renunciation of Freemasonry.

To men, to minds, to hearts, like these coming up in their devotions to our altars from all times and from all countries, Masonry may proudly point, as Cornelia did of old to her children and say, indeed with truth, "These - these are my jewels."

One hundred years have elapsed since George Washington knelt at the sacred altar of Masonry, as an humble thirster after knowledge, and then and there imposed upon himself those solemn vows of obedience, and fidelity, and fraternity, which entitled him to the reception of our mystic light. A century has, since then, been irrevocably absorbed in the measureless abyss of time - and a century, how full of wonderful events. How many old empires have passed away, and how many new ones have been ushered into existence - how many dynasties of kings and Kaisers have been blotted from the herald book of history, and how many others have been inscribed upon its pages of mundane glory! How many of the wise and the good, the noble and the great, have drifted in the shattered bark of life to the "shores where all is dumb!" How in that great century, now forever gone, has "Man put forth His pomp, his pride, his skill, And arts that made fire, flood and earth, The vassals of his will."

How many hearts that then beat with all the hopes of youth, or with all the ambition of age, have ceased to pulsate - and all their throbs of love and joy, or hate and grief, been stilled in the silence of the tomb! What millions of that busy throng who then peopled the earth's surface have buried all their struggles and found a certain rest for all their varied labors in the grave! What revolutions have there not been in nations; what changes in art and science; how many old theories have been proved to be fallacious; how many new ones invested with truth, since that memorable evening, when George Washington was initiated into our sacred rites!

And he, too, with all his energy and endurance; with all his wisdom and purity; with all his power and popularity - even he has passed away - has gone from us forever, leaving his glory and his virtues as a legacy to his country.

But time, which has thus drawn into the vortex of its mighty gulf, the perishable fabrics of man's device, and buried in one common wreck - the inventors and their inventions - the players and the stage on which they strutted their "brief hour," has beaten in vain, with all its rolling billows against the impregnable rock of Masonry.

Though other things have passed away, that still remains; now as it has ever been - indissoluble - immutable - no landmark subverted-no fragment dissevered from its perfect mass; its columns still standing in strong support; its lights still burning with undiminished splendor; its altars still blazing with their sacred fires; its truth still pure as in the day of its birth hood; and when the cycle of another century shall have revolved, and you and I, and all that are elsewhere meeting on this festival day, shall have gone down to the dust from whence we sprung - another generation will be here - again to meet upon a second jubilee, and with like hopes and joys, and with like words of granulation and songs of triumph, to celebrate the two hundredth anniversary of that day which gave to Masonry the noblest of her sons, in him who was *"First in war, first in peace, and first in the hearts of his countrymen."*

The Testimony of President George Washington

Masons love to dwell on the fact that the illustrious Father of his country, was a brother Mason. They feel that under the panoply of his great name, they may securely bid defiance to the bitter charges of malignity. They know that the world is conscious that Washington, to quote the language of Clinton, "would not have encouraged an institution hostile to morality, religion, good order, and the public welfare."

Many testimonials of the good opinion entertained by Washington of the masonic society, of which he had been a member from early life, are on record; a few however, will suffice to demonstrate that Freemasons do not boast too much, when they claim him as the undeviating friend and adherent of the institution.

In answer to a complimentary address, when President of the United States, from the officers and members of King David's Lodge in Rhode-Island, he said:

"Being persuaded that a just application of the principles on which the masonic fraternity is founded, must be promotive of private virtue and public prosperity, I shall always be happy to advance the interest of the society and to be considered by them a deserving brother."

In 1792, the Grand Lodge of Massachusetts dedicated to him its Book of Constitutions. and in replying to the communication of the fact, he still more distinctly announces his favorable opinion of Free masonry, in the following sentences:

"Flattering as it may be to the human mind, and truly honorable as it is, to receive from our fellow citizens, testimonies of approbation, for exertions to promote the public welfare, it is not less pleasing to know, that the milder virtues of the heart are highly respected by a society, whose liberal principles are founded on the immutable laws of truth and justice.

"To enlarge the sphere of social happiness is worthy of the beautiful design of a masonic institution; and it is most fervently to be wished, that the conduct of every member of the fraternity, as was those publications that discover the principles which actuate them, may tend to convince mankind that the grand object of Masonry is to promote the happiness of the human race."

That our beloved brother continued through life to entertain these favorable opinions of the masonic institution, will be evident from the following expression contained in a reply made by him to the Grand Lodge of Massachusetts in April 1798, not three years before his death.

"My attachment," he says, "to the society of which we are members, will dispose me always to contribute my best endeavors to promote the honor and interest of the craft."

For the following explicit expression of what may be supposed to be the last published opinion of Washington, as to the character of the masonic institution, we are indebted to the researches of Charles Gilman, Esq., Grand Master of the Grand Lodge of Maryland. It is to be found in an extract from a letter written to the Grand Lodge of Maryland, on the 8th November 1798, only thirteen months before his death. The original is contained in the archives of that body, and a copy has lately been published for the first time in Moore's Freemasons' Monthly Magazine." The letter commences as follows:

"Gentlemen and Brothers:—Your obliging and affectionate letter, together with a copy of the Constitutions of Masonry, has been put into my hands by your Grand Master, for which I pray you to accept my best thanks. So far as I am acquainted with the principles and doctrines of Freemasonry, I conceive them to be founded in benevolence, and to be exercised only for the good of mankind; I cannot therefore, upon this ground, withdraw my approbation from it."

Gen. Washington cultivated Masonry with sedulous attention. While Commander-in-chief of the army, he countenanced the establishment and encourage the labors of travelling Lodges among the military, considering them as schools of urbanity, well calculated to disseminate those mild virtues of the heart which are so ornamental to the human character, and so peculiarly fitted to alleviate the miseries of war. And notwithstanding the engrossing cares of his high station, he found frequent opportunities of visiting the Lodges, and participating in the labors of the craft.

The Hon. Timothy Bigelow delivered a eulogy on the character of Washington before the Grand Lodge of Massachusetts, on the 11th of February 1800, and at that period so near the date of his death, when authentic information could easily be obtained, and when it is scarcely probable that an erroneous statement of so important a nature would willfully have been made, Bigelow asserts on the authority of members of Washington's own Lodge, that he died the Master of a Lodge. Bigelow's language is as follows:

"The information received from our brethren, who had the happiness to be members of the Lodge over which he presided for many years, and of which he died the Master, furnishes us abundant proof of his persevering zeal for the prosperity of the institution. Constant and punctual in his attendance, scrupulous in his observance of the regulations of the Lodge, and solicitous at all times to communicate light and instruction, he discharged the duties of the chair with uncommon dignity and intelligence in all the mysteries of our art."

Washington was initiated into the mysteries of Freemasonry, on the 4th of November 1752 in Fredericksburg in Virginia; he received his second degree on the 3d of March, and his third on the 4th of August in the following year. This appears from the "Ledger" or Record Book of the Lodge, from which Brother Moore made the following extract when on a visit to Washington in 1848, to assist in the ceremonies of laying the corner stone of the Washington Monument.

"November 4, 5752,-Received of Mr. George Washington, for his entrance of 23."

"March 3, 5753,-George Washington passed Fellow Craft."

August 4, 5753,-George Washington raised Master Mason."

At Alexandria, Va., is contained the original Warrant of Constitution of Lodge No. 22, of which we have a right to presume that Washington was the first Master," from the fact that his name is first mentioned in the list of brethren, to whom the warrant was granted. Moore gives the following extract from this interesting document, which he copied some years ago from the original.

"I, Edward Randolph, Governor of the State, and Grand Master of the Grand Lodge of Virginia —Do hereby constitute and appoint our Illustrious and well-beloved Brother, GEORGE WASHINGTON, late General and Commander-in-Chief of the forces of the United States of America, and our worthy Brothers McCrea, William Hunter, Jr., and John Allison, Esq., together with all such other

Brethren as may be admitted to associate with them, be a just, true, and regular Lodge of Freemasons, by the name, title, and designation of the Alexandria Lodge, No. 22."

The name of this Lodge was changed, in 1805, to that of "Washington Alexandria Lodge." It is still in active operation, and occupied a distinguished place in the ceremonial of laying the corner stone of the Washington Monument, on the 4th of July, 1848.

These testimonials of the masonic life and opinions of the "Father of his country," are of inestimable value to the defense of the institution.— "They demonstrate," to use the language of brother Moore, "beyond controversy, his attachment to the institution—the high estimation in which he held its principles—his conviction of its ability to promote "private virtue and public prosperity.' And they place, beyond all doubt, his 'disposition always to contribute his best endeavors to promote the honor and interest of the craft'—a disposition which he continued to manifest, and on all proper occasions to avow, to the latest period of his life."

On September 12, 1789, in the New York Weekly Museum (a newspaper), the following poem was printed. While the poem's author is unknown, the subject of the poem is well-known to all Freemasons. The subject is our own beloved Wor. Bro. George Washington, America's most famous Freemason.

George Washington: An Acrostic

Great patron of our noble art divine,
Extend thy all enliv'ning orient ray,
On Masonry with ardent lustre shine,
Refulgent shine--and usher in new day;
Great architect, bright morning star of fame,
Each Mason glories in his patrons name.

What's great and good, and beautiful to see,
Are all compriz'd, and to be found in thee;
Statesman, hero, patriot, brother dear,
Humane, benevolent, just and sincere;
Intrepid soldier, guardian of our land,
Ne'er let us fall beneath oppressor's hand,
Gently lead and guide us on to fame,
That we may stand recorded with thy name;
On Mason's hearts thy name shall stand secure,
Nor be forgot while Masonry endures.

Appendix 1:
The Testimony of President John Adams

John Adams, the successor of George Washington in the Presidential Chair of the United States, and one of the most distinguished patriots in that eventful period of our history, which is emphatically described as having been "the time that tried men's souls," was himself no Mason, but he has publicly declared his favorable opinion of the character of the institution.

In the year 1798, the Grand Lodge of Massachusetts communicated an address to President Adams, in acknowledgement of the wisdom, firmness, and integrity, which had characterized his public conduct. To this address, Mr. Adams replied in a strain of encomium, which will surely more than compensate for the profound abuse, which subsequently, during a time of political excitement, was lavished upon the institution by John Quincy Adams, his son. The censure of the son, based upon false statements and unproved charges, will sink into oblivion—but the encomium of the father, founded on the experience and examples of his friends, the good and great men of the nation, will remain an enduring memorial of the virtuous character of our Order.

The reply of Mr. Adams, addressed to the Grand Lodge of Massachusetts, is in the following words.

"As I never had the honor to be one of your ancient fraternity, I feel myself under the greater obligations to you, for this affectionate and respectful address. Many of my best friends have been Masons, and two of them, my professional patron, the learned Gridley, and my intimate friend, your immortal Warren, whose life and death were lessons and examples of patriotism and philanthropy, were Grand Master; yet so it has happened, that I had never the felicity to be initiated. Such examples as these, and a greater still in my venerable predecessor, would have been sufficient, to induce me to hold the institution and fraternity in esteem and honor, as favorable to the support of civil authority, if I had not known their love of the fine arts, their delight in hospitality, and devotion to humanity.

"Your indulgent opinion of my conduct, and your benevolent wishes for the fortunate termination of my public labors, have my sincere thanks.

"The public engagement of your utmost exertions in the cause of your country, and the offer of your services to protect the fair inheritance of your ancestors, are proofs, that you are not chargeable with those designs, the imputation of which, in other parts of the world, has embarrassed the public mind, with respect to the real views of your society."

Appendix 2:
The Testimony of President Andrew Jackson

Of the early masonic history of Andrew Jackson but little is known. In a tribute to his memory, prepared by the Rev. Mr. Neeley, the Grand Chaplain of the Grand Lodge of Tennessee, it is stated that, in the early part of his life, he was connected with a Lodge that met at Clover Bottom, under the jurisdiction of the Grand Lodge of Kentucky. In the year 1822, he was elected and installed as Grand Master of Tennessee, and presided during the session of that year, with all the firmness and dignity which distinguished him in other situations of command. He was, in the subsequent year, reelected to this important position, and continued to exercise its functions with his usual promptitude and decision. He was connected with the Order until the time of his death, and had made some progress in the higher degrees, since we find him, but a few years previous to his death, assisting in the imposing ceremonies of installing the officers of Cumberland Royal Arch Chapter. The testimony of a man, whose public career was so intimately interwoven with the destinies of the nation, and whose private life was a beautiful illustration of benevolence, is too valuable to be omitted in a work, professedly intended to be a defense of Freemasonry.

In 1833, Gen. Jackson, while on a visit to Boston, was invited, by the Grand Lodge of Massachusetts, to visit them at a special communication to be called for that purpose. The

General made arrangements for doing so, but on the arrival of the evening was compelled to forego his intention, in consequence of excessive fatigue. He sent, however, a letter, in which he expressed his favorable wishes for the prosperity of the institution, as one "calculated to benefit mankind." The Hon. Joel R. Poinsett, one of the President's suite, attended the communication, and delivered the following message, in which the opinion entertained by Jackson of the institution, is explicitly stated.

"Most Worshipful Brother: The President of the United States has charged me to express to his brethren of the Grand Lodge of Massachusetts, his sincere regret at being prevented, by indisposition, from accepting their invitation to meet them in the temple, and from tendering to them, in person, his acknowledgments for their attentions. He begged me to assure them, that he shall ever feel a lively interest in the welfare of an institution, with which he has been so long connected, and whose objects are purely philanthropic; and he has instructed me to express to them the high esteem and fraternal regard which he cherishes for them all."

Appendix 3:
The Masonic Presidents

George Washington, First U.S. President, 1789-1797

George Washington served as the first President of the United States of America. He was inaugurated on April 30, 1789 and served two terms as President. Born in 1732, Washington was initiated on November 4, 1752, passed on March 3, 1753, and raised a Master Mason on August 4, 1753 in Fredericksburg Lodge, Virginia. He would serve as the Commander in Chief of the Continental Armies during the Revolutionary War. In 1788, Washington was appointed Charter Master of Alexandria Lodge No. 22, Virginia during the organization of the lodge and in December 1788, he was elected Master. There is no evidence that he was ever installed or presided over any meetings of this lodge. While President, he would act as Grand Master in leveling the cornerstone of the U.S. Capitol in Washington, D.C. on September 18, 1793. During his life, Washington was somewhat active and supportive of Freemasonry. He died on December 14, 1799, less than three years following his second term as President.

James Monroe, Fifth U.S. President, 1817-1825

James Monroe was born in Westmoreland County, Virginia in 1758. Monroe attended the College of William and Mary, fought with distinction in the Continental Army, and practiced law in Fredericksburg, Virginia. There is some dispute regarding the Masonic affiliation of Bro. Monroe due to the loss of lodge records. It appears that he was initiated on November 9, 1775 in St. John's Regimental Lodge in the Continental Army. He later affiliated with Williamsburg Lodge No. 6 in Williamsburg, Virginia. There are no known records to confirm his advancement through the degrees but there is evidence that Monroe was received as a Master Mason during a visit to a Tennessee lodge in 1819. It is interesting to note that Bro. Monroe was not yet eighteen when initiated indicating the concept of "lawful age" had not been universally fixed at twenty-one at this time. Like Washington, Monroe would serve two terms as President. He died on July 4, 1831 in New York.

Andrew Jackson, Seventh U.S. President, 1829-1837

Born in the backwoods settlement of Waxhaw, South Carolina on March 15, 1767, Andrew Jackson received sporadic education. But in his late teens he read law for about two years, and he became an outstanding young lawyer in Tennessee. Fiercely jealous of his honor, he engaged in brawls, and in a duel killed a man who cast an unjustified slur on his wife Rachel. A major general in the War of 1812, Jackson became a national hero when he defeated the British at New Orleans. The Masonic record of Brother Jackson has not been located though there is no doubt he was a Mason. He appears to have been a member of St. Tammany Lodge No. 29, Nashville, Tennessee, as early as 1800. The lodge name was later changed to Harmony Lodge No. 1 on November 1, 1800. Brother Jackson is officially listed as a member in the Lodge Returns to the Grand Lodge of Tennessee for 1805. Very active in Freemasonry, Brother Jackson was a Grand Master of Masons in Tennessee, serving from October 1822 until October 1824. Jackson served two terms as President from 1829 until 1837. He died on June 8, 1845 at the Hermitage near Nashville, Tennessee.

James K. Polk, Eleventh U.S. President, 1845-1849

James K. Polk was born in Mecklenburg County, North Carolina, on November 2, 1795. Studious and industrious, Polk was graduated with honors in 1818 from the University of North Carolina. As a young lawyer he entered politics, served in the Tennessee legislature, and became a friend of Andrew Jackson. Brother Polk was initiated in Columbia Lodge No. 31 on June 5, 1820 located in Columbia, Tennessee. He would be passed and raised in this lodge though the actual dates are unknown. In 1825 he was exalted a Royal Arch Mason in LaFayette Chapter No. 4 located in Columbia. Polk would serve as the Governor of Tennessee from 1839 through 1841 prior to his election as President of the United States. He would serve one term as President from 1845 to 1849. He left office in poor health and died a few months later on June 15, 1849 in Nashville, Tennessee.

James A. Buchanan, Fifteenth U.S. President, 1857-1861

Born in Cove Gap near Mercersburg, Pennsylvania into a well-to-do Pennsylvania family on April 23, 1791, James A. Buchanan, a graduate of Dickinson College, was gifted as a debater and learned in the law. Tall, stately, and stiffly formal, he was the only President who never married. Brother Buchanan was initiated on December 11, 1816, passed and raised in Lancaster Lodge No. 43 in Lancaster, Pennsylvania. He served as Master of his lodge from 1822 to 1823. In 1824, he was appointed District Deputy Grand Master for the Counties of Lancaster, Lebanon and York. His tenure as President was fraught with controversy surrounding the issues of states rights and slavery. Inaugurated in 1857, Buchanan retired from the Presidency after one term in office and returned to Lancaster, Pennsylvania where he died on June 1, 1868.

Andrew Johnson, Seventeenth U.S. President, 1865-1869

Born in Raleigh, North Carolina, on December 29, 1808, Johnson grew up in poverty. He was apprenticed to a tailor as a boy, but ran away. He opened a tailor shop in Greeneville, Tennessee, married Eliza McCardle, and participated in debates at the local academy. Entering politics, he became an adept stump speaker, championing the common man. Johnson became a Mason in 1851 when he was initiated, passed, and raised in Greenville Lodge No. 119 located at Greenville, Tennessee. Following the assassination of Abraham Lincoln in 1865, the Presidency fell upon Vice-President Johnson, an old-fashioned southern Jacksonian Democrat. Although an honest and honorable man, Andrew Johnson was one of the most unfortunate of Presidents. Arrayed against him were the Radical Republicans in Congress, brilliantly led and ruthless in their tactics. In 1867, the House of Representatives voted eleven articles of impeachment against him. He was tried by the Senate in the spring of 1868 and acquitted by one vote. While serving as President, he received the Scottish Rite degrees during 1867. Johnson left the White House in 1869 after serving almost four years as President completing Lincoln's second term. Johnson died on July 31, 1875 in Carter's Station, Tennessee.

James A. Garfield, Twentieth U.S. President, 1881

James A. Garfield was born in Cuyahoga County, Ohio, on November 19, 1831. Fatherless at two, he later drove canal boat teams, somehow earning enough money for an education. He was graduated from Williams College in Massachusetts in 1856, and he returned to the Western Reserve Eclectic Institute (later Hiram College) in Ohio as a classics professor. Within a year he was made its president. Garfield was initiated on November 19, 1861 in Magnolia Lodge No. 20 in Columbus, Ohio. Owing to Civil War duties, Brother Garfield did not receive the Third Degree until November 22, 1864 in Columbus Lodge No. 30 in Columbus, Ohio. On October 10, 1866, he affiliated with Garrettsville Lodge No. 246 in Garrettsville, Ohio. Brother Garfield became a Charter Member of Pentalpha Lodge No. 23 of Washington, D.C. on May 4, 1869. Garfield was elected President in 1880 by a margin of only 10,000 popular votes and was inaugurated on March 4, 1881. His Presidency was cut short when an embittered attorney who had sought a consular post shot him on July 2, 1881, in a Washington railroad station. Mortally wounded, Garfield died on September 19, 1881 from the gunshot wound.

William McKinley. Twenty-Fifth U.S. President, 1897-1901

Born in Niles, Ohio, on January 29, 1843, McKinley briefly attended Allegheny College, and was teaching in a country school when the Civil War broke out. Enlisting as a private in the Union Army, he was mustered out at the end of the war as a brevet major of volunteers. He studied law, opened an office in Canton, Ohio, and married Ida Saxton, daughter of a local banker. McKinley was initiated, passed, and raised in Hiram Lodge No. 21 located in Winchester, Virginia during 1865. He affiliated with Canton Lodge No. 60 in Canton, Ohio on 1867 and later demitted to become a Charter Member of Eagle Lodge No. 431, also in Canton. McKinley was elected Governor of Ohio in 1891 and served two terms from 1892 to 1896. He was inaugurated as President in 1897 and was elected to a second term in 1900. McKinley's second term as President came to a tragic end in September 1901. While attending the Pan-American Exposition in Buffalo, New York he was shot by a deranged man. McKinley would die eight days later on September 14, 1901, becoming the second Masonic President to be assassinated.

Theodore Roosevelt, Twenty-Sixth U.S. President, 1901-1909

With the assassination of President McKinley in 1901, Theodore Roosevelt, not quite 43, became the youngest President in the Nation's history. He brought new excitement and power to the Presidency as he vigorously led Congress and the American public toward progressive reforms and a strong foreign policy. He was born in New York City on October 27, 1858 into a wealthy family. Though he suffered from ill health as a youth, he was an avid outdoorsman and conservationist. During the Spanish-American War, Roosevelt was lieutenant colonel of the Rough Rider Regiment, which he led on a charge at the battle of San Juan. He was elected Governor of New York in 1898, serving with distinction. Assuming the Presidency in September 1901, Roosevelt received the three degrees in Matinecock Lodge No. 806 in Oyster Bay, New York during the year. He was very supportive of Freemasonry during the remainder of his life. Following the completion of McKinley's term, Roosevelt was elected to a second term in his own right and served as President through 1909. Roosevelt died on January 6, 1919 in Oyster Bay.

William H. Taft, Twenty-Seventh U.S. President, 1909-1913

William Howard Taft was born on September 15, 1857 in Cincinnati, Ohio, the son of a distinguished judge. He was graduated from Yale and returned to Cincinnati to study and practice law. He rose in politics through judiciary appointments earned through his own competence and availability. Brother Taft was made a "Mason at Sight" within the Body of Kilwinning Lodge No. 356 located in Cincinnati, Ohio on February 18, 1909. Taft's father and two brothers were also members of this Lodge. After the ceremony, Brother and President Taft addressed the Brethren, saying, "I am glad to be here, and to be a Mason. It does me good to feel the thrill that comes from recognizing on all hands the Fatherhood of God and the Brotherhood of Man." Taft was a distinguished jurist and an effective administrator but a poor politician. Large, jovial, and conscientious, Taft was inaugurated as President in 1909, and spent four uncomfortable years in the White House caught in the intense battles between the political factions of Washington. Taft's term ended in 1913 and, free of the Presidency, served as Professor of Law at Yale until Brother and President Warren G. Harding made him Chief Justice of the United States Supreme Court, a position he held until just before his death on March 8, 1930 in Washington, D.C.

Warren G. Harding, Twenty-Ninth U.S. President, 1921-1923

Warren G. Harding was born near Marion, Ohio, on November 2, 1865. An active civic leader, he became the publisher of a newspaper. He was a trustee of the Trinity Baptist Church, a director of almost every important business, and a leader in fraternal organizations and charitable enterprises. Harding was initiated in Freemasonry on June 28, 1901 in Marion Lodge No. 70 located in Marion, Ohio. Because of some personal antagonism, Brother Harding's advancement was hindered until 1920, by which time he had been nominated for President. Friends persuaded the opposition to withdraw the objection, and on August 27, 1920, nineteen years after his initiation, Brother Harding achieved the Sublime Degree of Master Mason in Marion Lodge. Harding won the Presidential election of 1920 by an unprecedented landslide of 60 percent of the popular vote. By 1923 the post World War I depression was giving way to a new wave of prosperity and newspapers proclaimed Harding as a wise statesman. However, word began to reach Harding that some of his friends were using their official positions for personal enrichment. This alarmed and worried Harding but he feared the political repercussions of exposing the scandals. Looking wan and depressed, Harding journeyed westward in the summer of 1923 carrying the burden of revealing the corruption. Unfortunately, he did not live to find out how the public would react to the scandals of his administration. On August 2, 1923, Harding died in San Francisco of a heart attack.

Franklin D. Roosevelt, Thirty-Second U.S. President, 1933-1945

Franklin D. Roosevelt was born on January 30, 1882 at Hyde Park, New York. He attended Harvard University and Columbia Law School. On St. Patrick's Day, 1905, he married Eleanor Roosevelt. Roosevelt entered public service through politics, serving in several state and federal positions before being elected Governor of New York in 1928. In the summer of 1921, at the age of 39, he was stricken with poliomyelitis. Demonstrating indomitable courage, Roosevelt fought to regain the use of his legs, particularly through swimming. Roosevelt received the three degrees in Masonry within Holland Lodge No. 8 located in New York City in 1911. During his lifetime he was supportive of Freemasonry and somewhat active in the fraternity. He was elected President in November 1932 to the first of four terms spanning the Great Depression to World War II. His tenure as President was a period of great social and political change in the United States. Assuming the Presidency at the depth of the Great Depression, he brought hope to the American people as he promised prompt, vigorous action, and asserted in his Inaugural Address, "the only thing we have to fear is fear itself." When the Japanese attacked Pearl Harbor on December 7, 1941, Roosevelt directed organization of the Nation's manpower and resources for global war. During this period he directed the war effort but also contemplated the planning of a United Nations in which international difficulties could be resolved. As the war drew to a close, Roosevelt's health deteriorated, and on April 12, 1945, while at Warm

Springs, Georgia, he died of a cerebral hemorrhage at the beginning of his fourth term as President.

Harry S. Truman, Thirty-Third U.S. President, 1945-1953

Harry S. Truman was born in Lamar, Missouri, in 1884. He grew up in Independence, and for 12 years prospered as a Missouri farmer. He went to France during World War I as a captain in the Field Artillery. Returning, he married Elizabeth Virginia Wallace, and opened a haberdashery in Kansas City. A very active Freemason, Truman received his Masonic degrees in Belton Lodge No. 450 in Grandview, Missouri in 1909. In 1911, Truman and several other Masons organized Grandview Lodge No. 618 and Truman served as the first Master of the Lodge. In 1940, Truman was elected Grand Master of the Grand Lodge of Missouri and would serve as such until October 1941. Truman became a U.S Senator in 1934 and was active in monitoring the war effort while in the Senate. Brother Franklin D. Roosevelt chose Truman to be his Vice-Presidential candidate in the 1944 elections, which Roosevelt won. During his few weeks as Vice President, Truman scarcely saw President Roosevelt, and received no briefing on the development of the atomic bomb or the unfolding difficulties with Soviet Russia. Suddenly these and a host of other wartime problems became Truman's to solve when, on April 12, 1945, he became President upon the death of Roosevelt. He told reporters, "I felt like the moon, the stars, and all the planets had fallen on me." As President, Truman made some of the most crucial decisions in history. Soon after V-E Day, the war against Japan had reached its final stage. An urgent plea to Japan to surrender was rejected. Truman, after consultations with his advisers, ordered atomic bombs dropped on cities devoted to war work. Two were Hiroshima and Nagasaki. The Japanese surrender quickly followed in 1945. In 1948, campaigning against the backdrop of crises in foreign affairs around the globe, Truman won a term as President in his own right. Deciding not to run for a second term, Truman retired from the Presidency in 1953 and returned to Independence, Missouri where he died on December 26, 1972 at the age of 88.

Gerald R. Ford, Thirty-Eighth U.S. President, 1974-1977

Born in Omaha, Nebraska, in 1913, Gerald R. Ford grew up in Grand Rapids, Michigan. He starred on the University of Michigan football team, and then went to Yale where he served as assistant coach while earning his law degree. During World War II he attained the rank of lieutenant commander in the Navy. After the war he returned to Grand Rapids, where he began the practice of law, and entered Republican politics. In 1948 he was elected to Congress where he developed a reputation for integrity and openness. That reputation made him popular during his twenty-five years in Congress where he served as House Minority Leader from 1965 to 1973. Ford was initiated in Freemasonry on September 30, 1949 in Malta Lodge No. 465 in Grand Rapids, Michigan. In 1951 he was received, passed and raised a Master Mason in Columbia Lodge No. 3 in Washington, D.C. as a courtesy for Malta Lodge while Ford served in Congress. When Ford took the oath of office as President on August 9, 1974, he declared, "I assume the Presidency under extraordinary circumstances.... This is an hour of history that troubles our minds and hurts our hearts." It was indeed an unprecedented time. He had been the first Vice President chosen under the terms of the Twenty-fifth Amendment and, in the aftermath of the Watergate scandal, was succeeding the first President ever to resign. President Ford won the Republican nomination for the Presidency in 1976, but lost the election to his Democratic opponent.

www.ingramcontent.com/pod-product-compliance
Lightning Source LLC
LaVergne TN
LVHW041459070426
835507LV00009B/697